ISBN: 1441447385

Copyright © 2009 Karen V. Penn

Published by VirtuousArt

Brockton, MA

USA

http //www.virtuousart.com

This book is dedicated to
all our grandchildren.

Love always,

Grandpa & Grandma Nawnie

Jesus never makes a promise,
that He can't keep.

Cuz He told me in His Word,
He won't leave me.

Jesus never makes a promise,
that He can't keep.

Yes He told me in His Word,
I'll be redeemed.

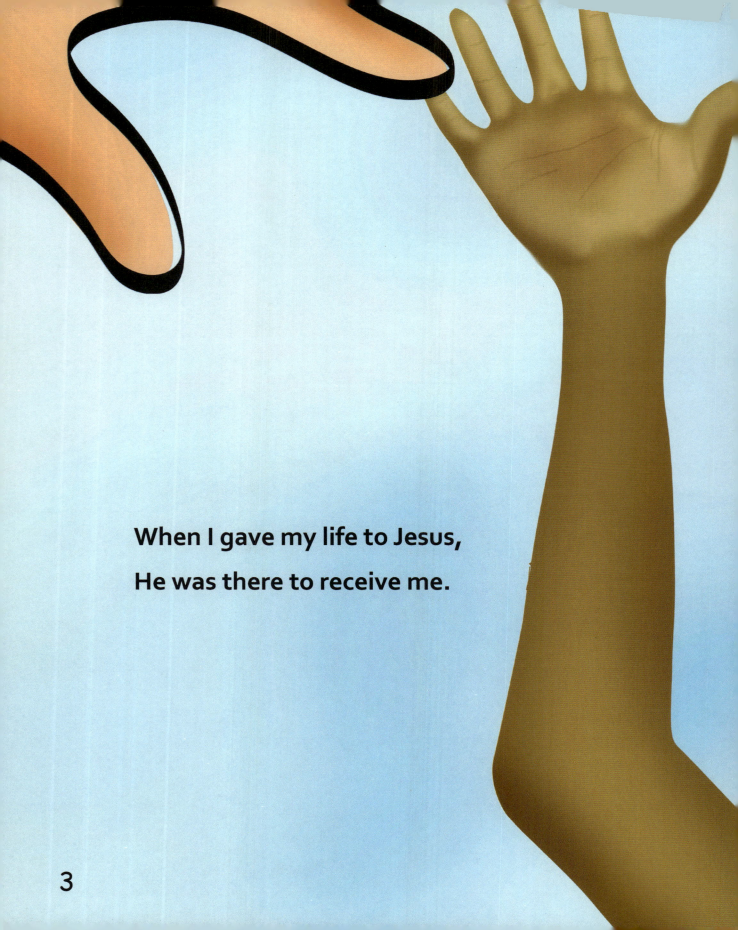

When I gave my life to Jesus,

He was there to receive me.

3

And He told me in His Word,

He'd never leave nor forsake me.

If I trust and never doubt,

in what the Holy Spirit tells me,

This I know . . .

He will always bring me out and,

And I trust to let Jesus do the rest.

4

5

Jesus never makes a promise,
that He can't keep.

Cuz He told me in His Word,
He won't leave me.

Jesus never makes a promise,
that He can't keep.

Yes He told me in His Word,
I'd be redeemed.

Don't you worry about your

trials and troubles.

Just give them over to Him.

You need to practice what you preach,

have a little faith,

this I know the Lord's gonna work them.

It's not easier said than done.

Here's the thing you must do.

This is all you gotta do.

Casting all your cares on Jesus.

This I know . . .

He'll bring you through . . .

Yes he will . . . Yes he will.

Jesus never makes a promise,

that He can't keep.

Cuz He told me in His Word,

He won't leave me.

Jesus never makes a promise,

That He can't keep.

Yes He told me in His Word,

I'll be redeemed.

Jesus never, makes a promise,

To you and me that he can't keep.

He is standing, and He's knocking,

Won't you answer, and let him in?

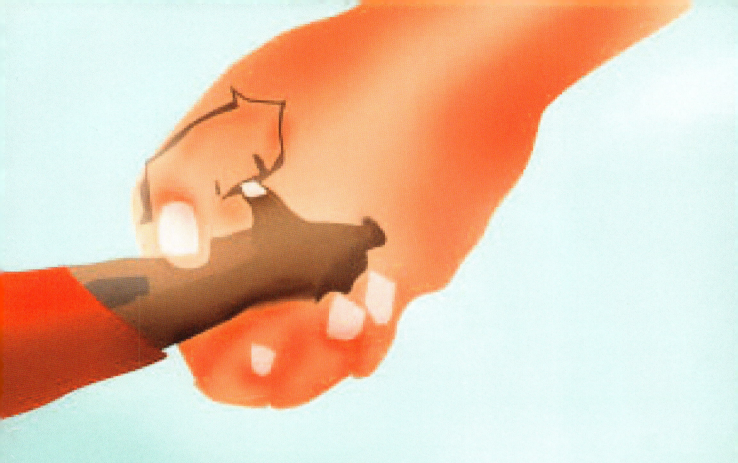

Jesus never, makes a promise,

To you and me that he can't keep.

Oh He's standing, and he's knocking

Won't you answer, and let him in?

Jesus never, makes a promise

To you and me that he can't keep.

He is standing, and He's knocking

Won't you answer, and let him in?

Jesus always keeps his promise (repeat)

20

The End.

Coloring Section

Enjoy coloring, framing and
hanging up your pictures.

Jesus never makes a promise that
he can't keep.

He will always
bring us out,

If we trust and
never doubt.

He told us in His Word that
He won't . . . leave.

Don't you worry about your
trials and troubles,
Just give them over to Him.

You have to practice what
you preach,
and have a little faith.

He told us in His Word that
we would be redeemed.

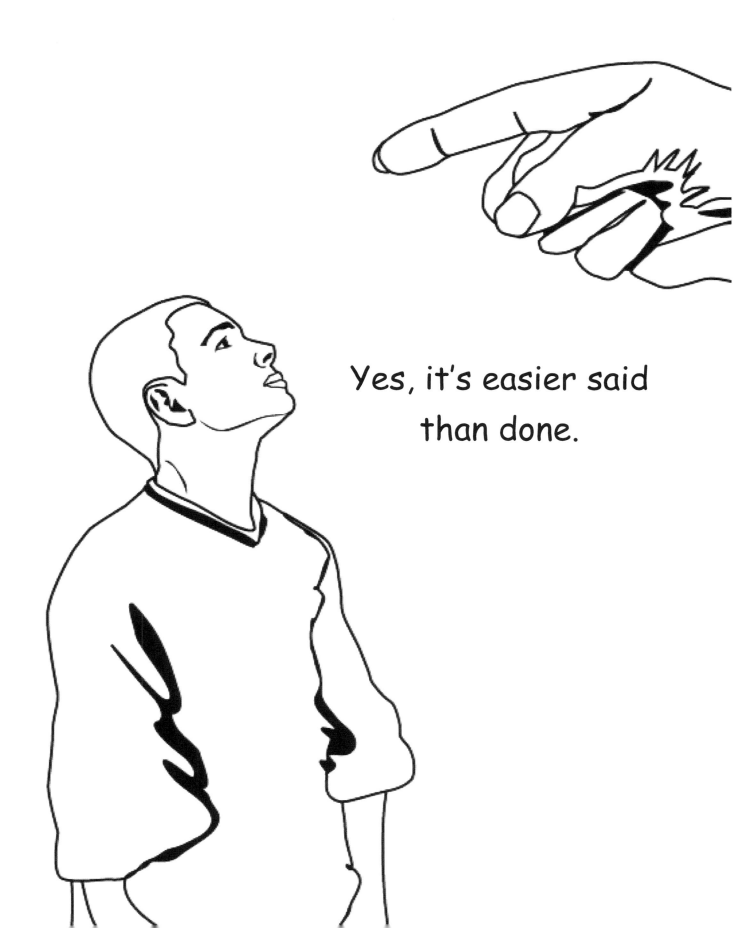

Yes, it's easier said than done.

He will bring you through.

Yes, He told us in His Word that we would be redeemed.

To purchase additional copies of
THIS BOOK AND the
sing-a-long CD send your request to:

VirtuousArt@comcast.net

To listen to samples or to purchase the entire music CD go to:

http://home.napster.com/ns/music/artist.html?
artist_id=12383260

To contact the author or illustrator go to:

VirtuousArt@comcast.net

Made in the USA